THE MINISTER AND MONEY

LAIDE ODUSOTE

Unless otherwise indicated, all scripture quotations are taken from the King James Version of the Bible.

ISBN: 9798842924653

Table of Contents

DEDICATION 5

FOREWORD 7

INTRODUCTION 11

Chapter One 15

THE MINISTER 15

Chapter Two 27

PERSONAL FINANCIAL HANDLING 27

Chapter Three 45

USING THE PULPIT ARIGHT 45

Chapter Four 59

THE 'NEVERS' OF THE PULPIT 59

About the Author 83

DEDICATION

I dedicate this book to all servants of God, who through their allegiance to Christ and his course, are doggedly spending and being spent for the kingdom.

These are true heroes of the faith!

FOREWORD

We currently live at a time when material wealth, money and all that money can buy are seen as evidences of success in ministry or signs of God's blessings to a believer in Christ Jesus. This reminds me of the Laodecian church in the "Apostolic age" who boasted and took comfort in her wealth, not knowing that God viewed her differently, as wretched and naked. This church in Asia minor had fallen into the trap of deceitfulness of riches but she was not aware of it. The Lord to them: "Because you say, 'I am rich, have become wealthy, and have need of nothing'—and do not know that you are wretched, miserable, poor, blind, and naked— Revelation 3:17 NKJV

Additionally, we also live at a time in church history, a precarious one at that, when people's motivation to serve God is what they can gain or have, chief among which is money. The most unfortunate part of this situation is that Christians did not just arrive at this state on their own. The leaders of the people had put them up to it. Much like Aaron, who was a leader among the people in the wilderness, misled them, erected a golden calf in the wilderness and presented it to the them as the god that brought them out of slavery in Egypt, many leaders in today's church are guilty of presenting material wealth (and money) as the god that people now gather to worship.

Anywhere they see material wealth, they believe that God is there. While they think that they gather to worship God, what many do, unknown to them, is to dance around gold. Gold, being the greatest store of wealth or value of all times, is symbolic of material wealth. Many have mistaken God for gold. But God is not gold and gold is not God. One is the creator and the other is a creature.

Without a doubt, money is one necessity that we would all have to constantly interact with in our personal lives and the work of ministry. However, because it presents such a propensity to master or control people and damn their souls, it becomes crucial for us as Christians and Christian leaders alike to know how to relate with it in order not to get trapped in its deceitfulness.

FOREWORD

In this small book, pastor Laide Odusote has made a bold attempt to challenge the status quo and put money in proper perspective. He presents, in an orderly and concise fashion, what our attitude to money must be, as stewards and beneficiaries of the manifold grace of God. This book is a must-read for any serious-minded Christian who is keen on doing things God's way and all Christian leaders who love the Lord and daily live with the consciousness of the fact that, one day, they will have to give an account of their stewardship before God.

Dr Odusote is a medical practitioner by secular training and a pastor by calling. He is one servant of Christ who has taught volumes upon volumes of messages bordering on new testament- Christian realities and there is no ambiguity about where he stands when it comes to defending the truth of the gospel and sticking to scriptural standards in words and in deed. I have the honour to write this foreword.

Dr Ninyo Omidiji

THE MINISTER AND MONEY

INTRODUCTION

Sitting down to write a book is one of the toughest works I've had to do. Therefore, writing this book only explains the gravity of the content I believe the Master will have me to share with His body.

It all started when I gave a message on "The Minister and Money" at our church's monthly "Arrow Heads Summit" (A monthly programme for church leaders). After going through my writings on it and being encouraged by a pastor friend as to putting this teaching in a book, it became more compelling to me to share with the body of Christ that which the Lord has graciously given to me over the years of my personal walk with Him.

Being able to communicate with other servants of God across the globe is borne out of my years of learning, studying, failing forward, observations, participation, questioning and challenging status quo. Personally, I strongly believe that if there's any aspect of ministerial balance we God's servants need to strike, it is our transaction with money and all it can bring!

The fall of man in Adam has so affected man that his relationship with money has always tilted to materialism and vain externalism. And so as God's stewards, being circumspect in the way we interface with material universe without subverting the gospel put into our trust becomes very critical.

Perusing the scriptures, going through the history of the church and considering today's church, one will be playing naivety, if the issue of our relationship with money is not wisely and prudently confronted, knowing fully well that how we handle such in our private and public life as God's servants can either be to the advance of God's kingdom or outright betrayal of trust.

Also, the ineluctable reality of our standing before the Master some day in judgment of how well we did the assignment committed unto our hands will make the wise minister of the gospel today to do God's work with sobriety and gravity. Like Paul said "Knowing therefore the terror of the Lord" 2Cor.5:11a

INTRODUCTION

My longing is that you and I will truly use all our God-given resources to advance a cause that is not just relevant in time but in all eternity to come.

I therefore challenge you to read this book that is really about scriptural expositions on how we, ministers should relate with and handle money to the end that the ministry be not blamed. And that through our individual ministries, the kingdom of God and His Christ will flourish.

This book will challenge your assumptions, belief system, general and acceptable teachings. But as wise saints of God, I enjoin you to check the scriptures yourself with sincerity and open heartedness and embrace change as the need arises.

Laide Odusote

THE MINISTER AND MONEY

Chapter One

THE MINISTER

But as we were allowed of God to be put in trust with the gospel, even so we speak; not as pleasing men; but God which trieth our hearts. (1 Thessalonians 2:4)

Let a man so account of us, as of the ministers of Christ, and stewards of the mysteries of God. (1 Corinthians 4:1)

Since the creation of man, God has always made His plan known and executed His pleasures through certain men that were called and specially graced for such. Examples of these men abound in the scriptures. From Adam, Noah, Abraham, Moses, Joseph, David, to Jesus and His disciples as you consider names. In terms of offices- these include; Prophets, Kings, Judges, Pastors, etc.

However, you may look at it, men have always been conscripted for a cause heavier than them and always heaven-ward!

Reasoning along with Paul the Apostle, our concern is to consider the New Testament ministers and how such should interface with money in order to faithfully execute God's pleasure as they joyfully submit to Him in the building of His people.

Who also hath made us able ministers of the new testament; not of the letter, but of the spirit: for the letter killeth, but the spirit giveth life. (2 Corinthians 3:6)

This book will help ministers of the New Testament to carefully relate with money and all it can bring.

CHOSEN OUT OF THE PACK

Looking at Luke 6: 12-13,

And it came to pass in those days, that he went out into a mountain to pray, and continued all night in prayer to God.

And when it was day, he called unto him his disciples: and of them he chose twelve, whom also he named apostles;

We saw how Jesus having communed with God in prayers chose the Apostles out of his disciples. So his ministers were chosen out of the pack. Any minister of the gospel of a necessity must first be a Christian then a servant of God! This probably looks simplistic but the reality is that no minister of the gospel must outgrow the fact that he is primarily a Christian and as such should model the Christ-life before other saints of God.

1 Timothy 4:11 -12,

Let no man despise thy youth; but be thou an example of the believers, in word, in conversation, in charity, in spirit, in faith, in purity.

As ministers of the gospel, we must not ignore the fact that living the Christian life before all must be our continual pursuit, it is out of this that true ministry flows.

By the reason of the new birth, with inner invasion with God's life in His Christ, one is a child of God baptized into the body of Christ by the Holy Spirit.

Based on God's choice, certain of the saints are chosen to become ministers of the gospel.

Ephesians 3:7-8,

Whereof I was made a minister, according to the gift of the grace of God given unto me by the effectual working of his power.

Unto me, who am less than the least of all saints, is this grace given, that I should preach among the Gentiles the unsearchable riches of Christ.

In this first a Christian then a minister experience, other saints can attest to the fact that one is truly a member of God's family.

Paul's conversion and entrance into the pack exemplify this.

Acts 9:26-27,

And when Saul was come to Jerusalem, he assayed to join himself to the disciples: but they were all afraid of him, and believed not that he was a disciple.

But Barnabas took him, and brought him to the apostles, and declared unto them how he had seen the Lord in the way, and that he had spoken to him, and how he had preached boldly at Damascus in the name of Jesus.

SEPARATED UNTO THE GOSPEL

Romans 1:1,

Paul, a servant of Jesus Christ, called to be an apostle, separated unto the gospel of God.

In 1 Thessalonians 2:4,

But as we were allowed of God to be put in trust with the gospel, even so we speak; not as pleasing men, but God, which trieth our hearts.

2 Timothy 1:11,

Whereunto I am appointed a preacher, and an apostle, and a teacher of the Gentiles.

Paul like other ministers, Peter and John used the rest of their lives to preach, teach and minister the gospel of our Lord Jesus Christ.

To do this effectively, the true minister must learn what the gospel is continually as made known through the "Law and the prophets".

Romans 16:25-26,

Now to him that is of power to stablish you according to my gospel, and the preaching of Jesus Christ, according to the revelation of the mystery, which was kept secret since the world began,

But now is made manifest, and by the scriptures of the prophets, according to the commandment of the everlasting God, made known to all nations for the obedience of faith:

All the ramifications of the gospel in its power and wisdom to save the lost and get the saints established in Christ and continually grow up into Him in all things must be known by the minister and he must relentlessly preach the same.

Sometimes, I'm tempted to believe that many of us ministers of the gospel don't realize the enormity of what is committed to our hands in the way we get excited about what we call benefits in ministry.

I believe, this is the gravest work any man can undertake on earth because it determines the eternal destiny of men and the fruitfulness of that which Jesus Christ gave His life for. Any wonder the apostle said in

Act 20: 24,

But none of this things move me, neither count I my life dear unto myself, so that I might finish my course with joy, and the ministry, which I have received of the grace of God.

Fellow servant of God, being trusted with the mysteries of the gospel of grace of God in Christ requires hard work, diligent study, qualitative and quantitative praying, money mastery and disciplined life style in order that you and I might make most of this assignment.

ALWAYS GROWING:

Peter told us to grow in grace and in the knowledge of our Lord Jesus Christ (2 Peter 3:18). Continual growth position the servant of God to model true Christianity before the saints and to make the truth known in a more powerful, skillful and pragmatic ways.

However, while growth is a natural occurrence, it requires embracing certain spiritual disciplines unyieldingly. These disciplines include what the Apostles prescribed for themselves in Acts 6:4, *'but we will give ourselves continually to prayer and to the ministry of the word'*.

Qualitative and quantitative praying is a must for anyone called to preach the gospel and make godly success out of it.

In one of the minister's meeting I attended recently, I made an observation of how some of the ministers present could not sustain qualitative praying. This I believe needs urgent attention if our ministries must become truly effective.

Rugged and sustained study of the scriptures that reveals Christ as the substance of the bible in both testaments, must be embraced.

Luke 24:27, 44:

[27]*And beginning at Moses and all the prophets, he expounded unto them in all the scriptures the things concerning himself.*

[44]*And he said unto them, These are the words which I spake unto you, while I was yet with you, that all things must be fulfilled, which were written in the law of Moses, and in the prophets, and in the psalms, concerning me.*

Colossians 1: 22-28,

In the body of his flesh through death, to present you holy and unblameable and unreproveable in his sight:

If ye continue in the faith grounded and settled, and be not moved away from the hope of the gospel, which ye have heard, and which was preached to every creature which is under heaven; whereof I Paul am made a minister;

Who now rejoice in my sufferings for you, and fill up that which is behind of the afflictions of Christ in my flesh for his body's sake, which is the church:

Whereof I am made a minister, according to the dispensation of God which is given to me for you, to fulfil the word of God;

Even the mystery which hath been hid from ages and from generations, but now is made manifest to his saints:

To whom God would make known what is the riches of the glory of this mystery among the Gentiles; which is Christ in you, the hope of glory:

Whom we preach, warning every man, and teaching every man in all wisdom; that we may present every man perfect in Christ Jesus:

2 Cor.4: 5,

'For we preach not ourselves, but Christ Jesus the Lord; and ourselves your servants for Jesus' sake.

Learning from other saints through reading of solid books, listening to sound teachings by other servants of God is also profitable, and must be embraced.

The summary of these is that, if one truly desires to do solid ministry, continual personal growth must be coveted, embraced and pursued unflinchingly.

PUTTING HUMAN NEEDS IN PROPER PERSPECTIVES

In a world, where what we shall eat or drink, building of houses and using good things of life is the drive of average man (Mathew 6: 3132) and in possessing much of these is your success measured. Getting out of such entanglement is only meant for men who are from another world and ready to live by the standard of the world from which they came.

Incidentally, this should be true of any saint of God who lives in this present world where acquisition, possession and obsessive materialism is the common denominator of all.

As a man, the minister of the gospel has legitimate human needs like other men, but he must be circumspect so that he is not distracted by these to the point that they become the object of his pursuit or means of assessment of his success in ministry. He must model before God's people that a man's life is more than eating and drinking and enjoying the good things of this life.

Therefore, take no thought, saying, what shall we eat? or, what shall we drink? or, Wherewithal shall we be clothed?

(For after all these things do the Gentiles seek:) for your heavenly Father knoweth that ye have need of all these things. (Matthew 6: 31-33)

We eat, drink, wear good clothes, live in good environment, drive good cars, etc. in order to live and advance God's course on earth and not the other way round.

The Daniels in Babylon - which is a picture of the saints in the fallen world - did not allow the food (pleasure) of Babylon to distract them from serving the interest of Jehovah in a strange land. While they ate, they knew they were not there to eat but to represent, serve and glorify their God.

This also must be burnt into our consciousness that enjoying the comfort of the riches of this world is never our goal but representing, serving and bringing glory to God. This we'll do regardless of the situation and circumstances we might be exposed to.

Chapter Two

PERSONAL FINANCIAL HANDLING

For our rejoicing is this, the testimony of our conscience, that in simplicity and godly sincerity, not with fleshly wisdom, but by the grace of God, we have had our conversation in the world, and more abundantly to you-ward. (2 Corinthians 1:12)

Let your moderation be known unto all men. The Lord is at hand. (Philippians 4:5)

Every minister must avoid the tendency of becoming a professional preacher like the scribes and

Pharisees Jesus rebuked in Matthew 23:2-3 saying,

The scribes and the Pharisees sit in Moses' seat:

All therefore whatsoever they bid you observe, that observe and do; but do not ye after their works: for they say, and do not.

For they teach and instruct other men, yet their lives did not model what they taught. The true ministers of the gospel must model the fact that the same gospel they preach is what they live by and as such become examples of the believers.

1 Timothy 4:12,

Let no man despise thy youth; but be thou an example of the believers, in word, in conversation, in charity, in spirit, in faith, in purity...

The old saints told their followers to follow their examples as they followed Christ.

Philippians 3:17,

Brethren, be followers together of me, and mark them which walk so as ye have us for an ensample.

Philippians 4:9,

Those things, which ye have both learned, and received, and heard, and seen in me, do: and the God of peace shall be with you.

It is evident that in our personal financial handlings as God's servants, we are wittingly or unwittingly modelling a life before the saints of God. In other words, the gospel of grace must constantly be lived by us for others to see and emulate.

I'll consider some of the qualities a minister should consciously model before others. These qualities are borne out of the life of Christ in us that we constantly allow to shape how we interact with financial matters.

As citizens of heaven, we know that the scripture enjoins us to function as pilgrims and strangers in the midst of a world that has lost its moral compass.

1 Peter 2:11,

Dearly beloved, I beseech you as strangers and pilgrims, abstain from fleshly lusts, which war against the soul.

Ephesians 4:17,

This I say therefore, and testify in the Lord, that ye henceforth walk not as other Gentiles walk, in the vanity of their mind.

And so, functioning from a lifestyle which is found in Christ Jesus becomes the only alternative for the saints of God and for that matter God's servants.

SIMPLICITY

As God's servant, one's interaction with money and all it can bring reflects a quality of life that is borne out a consciousness that no earthly thing gives the saint any lasting advantage in life. With satisfaction in Christ alone, he thankfully enjoys the much or little that God brings his way. This manifests in all his human needs as eating, drinking, wearing clothes, building house, buying cars etc. Living a qualitative life in Christ Jesus to him is more than enjoying whatsoever is in this life.

In this state of renewed mind in Christ; complexes, high-mindedness, high-maintenance living, and all excesses of the flesh are conquered. With such men, wastage of earthly resources committed to their trust become impossible. They readily model moderation before all the saints.

Philippians 4:5,

Let your moderation be known unto all men. The Lord is at hand.

The virtue of simplicity in Christ, (2 Corinthians 11:2) is now the treasure such men treasure. Such servant of God will do much with little, relate with all men in love and be blessing to other saints and all men as they have opportunity.

Such simplicity characterized the old saints like Esther when she was to appear before King Ahasuerus, she was so contented with what was given to her by the King Chamberlain, Hegai. She declared by her action that her acceptability by the King was beyond what she could greedily grab by herself.

Esther 2:15,

Now when the turn of Esther, the daughter of Abihail the uncle of Mordecai, who had taken her for his daughter, was come to go in unto the king, she required nothing but what Hegai the king's chamberlain, the keeper of the women, appointed. And Esther obtained favour in the sight of all them that looked upon her.

The complexities in dressing, the much ado in make ups and other paraphernalia in dressing has so affected our world that the kingdom citizens are not spared in this self-conceit pursuits. The simplicity that women should be adorned with is lost in this world of complex splurging of fortune on artificialities.

But for the minister of the gospel, the incorruptible ornament in the hidden man of the heart is her true beauty, hence the secret of her simplicity!

1 Peter 3:2-3,

While they behold your chaste conversation coupled with fear. Whose adorning let it not be that outward adorning of plaiting the hair, and of wearing of gold, or of putting on of apparel.

GENEROSITY

To describe a servant of God as ungenerous is incongruous with the nature of Him whom we represent and preach.

I personally believe that if there is anything we servants of God have to live out, it is true generosity that seeks the progress of God's people and the world we are sent to save. I mean a generous heart that gives

altruistically and sacrificially as a result of the gracious working of God's Spirit in our hearts, empowering us to live the way the Master lived.

The Apostles modelled a life of true generosity in the way they gave to God's people.

Act 20:34,

Yea, ye yourselves know, that these hands have ministered unto my necessities, and to them that were with me.

Paul declared unequivocally that he would spend, and be spent for God's people and he will yet give to them as he sought not theirs but they themselves

2 Corinthians 12:14-15,

Behold, the third time I am ready to come to you; and I will not be burdensome to you: for I seek not yours, but you: for the children ought not to lay up for the parents, but the parents for the children.

And I will very gladly spend and be spent for you; though the more abundantly I love you, the less I be loved.

The erroneous teaching that makes us to belief that the saints should always give up i.e. "you give to the fathers" in order to be blessed, is not totally true, for the apostle 'gave down' to the people "the fathers laying up for the children".

2 Corinthians 12:14;

Behold, the third time I am ready to come to you; and I will not be burdensome to you: for I seek not yours, but you: for the children ought not to lay up for the parents, but the parents for the children.

Sometimes, what we, ministers of gospel say today contradicts what the Apostles taught and practiced. You hear things like, 'if you give to God's people, they won't develop their faith, they will now be dependent on the church'.

My question is "are we not dependent on their tithes, offering and other giving?" Or is the money we are using to build our ministry coming from heaven? Why did the Apostle give to God's people and were not afraid of the new truth we have discovered? Some also declared that what we owe God's people is the word, again I believe this is not the whole truth, we owe them the love that reflects in generous giving and teaching of sound doctrine.

An article was recently published in one of our dailies that examine how Senior Pastors/General Overseers remunerate pastors and church workers, it was obvious that in today's economy, what these men are paid is just too small, in comparison with their counterpart outside church work.

While I am not in any position to prescribe any specific amount as perks for our workers, I believe we need to be fair with God's people.

Colossians 4:1,

Masters, give unto your servants that which is just and equal; knowing that ye also have a Master in heaven.

James 5:1-5,

Go to now, ye rich men, weep and howl for your miseries that shall come upon you.

Your riches are corrupted, and your garments are motheaten.

Your gold and silver is cankered; and the rust of them shall be a witness against you, and shall eat your flesh as it were fire. Ye have heaped treasure together for the last days.

Behold, the hire of the labourers who have reaped down your fields, which is of you kept back by fraud, crieth: and the cries of them which have reaped are entered into the ears of the Lord of sabaoth.

Ye have lived in pleasure on the earth, and been wanton; ye have nourished your hearts, as in a day of slaughter.

With heavy monthly income in tithes and offering that come into our churches, I still wonder how a university graduate will still be paid so little. My question is what are we building? What do we want to do with all the money in the bank? What expansion of ministry are we making at the expense of God's people all because they have no choice? They have been put under bondage of 'they are serving God and not man'. Are their counterparts as civil servants and other employees or entrepreneurs serving devil? Unwittingly, we encourage stealing and cunning craftiness in the church because of our own hidden greed and selfishness.

The Apostles boasted, 'being poor making many rich', I hope ours will not be 'being rich, making many poor'.

Our giving as God's servant must transcend the self-driven giving done by men who do not know God, who give to get more in return, but embracing a love-driven giving spirit that sacrifices for the good of others.

Such behooves us if we are to live to the praise of God's glory.

INTEGRITY

David as God's servant fed God's people with the integrity of his heart and guided them by the skillfulness of his hands. Psalm 78:72

 Any wonder, the bible described him as a man who served his generation by the will of God.

Acts 13:36,

For David, after he had served his own generation by the will of God, fell on sleep, and was laid unto his fathers, and saw corruption:

To David, integrity (honesty, wholeness of heart, completeness, incorruptibility and soundness) was everything. By integrity, we refer to the adherence/upholding quality of life that stems from a heart that is in constant alignment with the truth found in Christ alone and as such compromise for sensual gains is not an option.

Hence, the private and public life of any minister of the gospel takes that form of living which upholds and celebrates richness of heart in Christ as the ultimate gain. All servants of God in the scriptures had to be tried by heaven to reveal their innate drive whether gain or God.

Balaam the prophet was tempted with gain by Balak and he fell for it, his dearth of integrity was revealed and till today he remains a warning example for the church as regards covetousness.

2 Peter 2:15-16,

Which have forsaken the right way, and are gone astray, following the way of Balaam the son of Bosor, who loved the wages of unrighteousness;

But was rebuked for his iniquity: the dumb ass speaking with man's voice forbad the madness of the prophet.

Solomon the king of Israel has the following to say in Proverbs 28:6,

Better is the poor that walketh in his uprightness, than he that is perverse in his ways, though he be rich.

Psalm 37:16,

A little that a righteous man hath is better than the riches of many wicked.

Proverbs 16:8,

Better is a little with righteousness than great revenues without right.

Our adherence to righteous living and true holiness checkmates continually every temptation to compromise our integrity. We speak loudly with our lives to our members that a little with integrity is better than so much without it.

Life in Christ is to be coveted, embraced dand lived out continually. As the Lord deems it fit to increase us financially, we are well informed that the pure state of our hearts that embraces the unsearchable riches of Christ is always the basis of our true gain. Ours is about quality of life in Christ Jesus shaping how we handle the quantity we get out of life!

To such servants of God, celebrating the quality of life in Christ is their drive and life pursuit and not the quantity of possessions made out of self-delusion. Judging then from this dimension of living, it is difficult to measure the success of a true servant of God who upholds integrity of heart by any worldly standard of possessions or positions.

How we also handle church fund or money committed to our trust must also reveal integrity. In handling the offering raised for the poor saints at Jerusalem, Paul handled the contribution transparently.

2 Corinthians 8: 18-21,

And we have sent with him the brother, whose praise is in the gospel throughout all the churches;

And not that only, but who was also chosen of the churches to travel with us with this grace, which is administered by us to the glory of the same Lord, and declaration of your ready mind:

Avoiding this, that no man should blame us in this abundance which is administered by us:

Providing for honest things, not only in the sight of the Lord, but also in the sight of men.

Let's do all ours with decency and honesty, the Lord is at hand.

CONTENTMENT AND TRUST

In a world that operates like the children of horseleach Proverbs 30:15 says,

The horseleach hath two daughters, crying, Give, give. There are three things that are never satisfied, yea, four things say not, it is enough:

The servants of Christ must be circumspect, otherwise such a one will be captured and tamed by covetousness.

As I relate with fellow Christians something unseemly standout among some of us, the greedy longing for more and the lack of satisfaction with God and that which He's graciously given to us.

God in His goodness, judgment and sovereign wisdom has distributed to all of us severally as He wills and it is important that we thankfully enjoy all that is given to us while we live to the praise and glory of His name. In order to live after this, God's servant must truly repose his confidence and trust in the good Lord, who declared He will never live nor forsake us.

Hebrews 13:5-6,

Let your conversation be without covetousness; and be content with such things as ye have: for he hath said, I will never leave thee, nor forsake thee.

So that we may boldly say, The Lord is my helper, and I will not fear what man shall do unto me.

Our lifestyle must be free of covetousness else contentment will be practically impossible. Each one of us must enjoy his present state in possession and position while we serve the Master's interest continually. The temptation of using the good things of life should not pressure us out of the present state we find ourselves with complaining and murmuring without a restful heart that serves the Master.

Whether the need for a good car, house, electronic gadgets, need of musical instruments, building of church auditorium, nothing on earth is worth pressuring us into a state of displeasure with our God.

"Godliness and contentment" is still a great gain – For we brought nothing into this world, and it is certain we can carry nothing out (1 Timothy 6:7).

We just need to be happy, pleasant, and grateful to God in our present state to have even granted us mercy to live and serve Him.

"he who is not contented with what he has would not be with what he would like to have" –said Socrates.

So dear servant of God, let the watching of your life by other saints reveal 'true definition of contentment'.

Chapter Three

USING THE PULPIT ARIGHT

But speak thou the things which become sound doctrine. (Titus 2:1)

And all thy children shall be taught of the Lord; and great shall be the peace of thy children. (Isaiah 54:13)

Nothing can or rather should be more exhilarating and fulfilling than seeing the members of one's church walking in the truth.

Grace be with you, mercy, and peace, from God the Father, and from the Lord Jesus Christ, the Son of the Father, in truth and love.

I rejoiced greatly that I found of thy children walking in truth, as we have received a commandment from the Father. (2 John vs 3-4)

Walking circumspectly as regards the relationship of the saints with money and all it can bring, should be the dogged quest of God's servants.

For this to be done, the minister of God must first be grounded in sound doctrine, and should skillfully and powerfully communicate the same to God's people continually to the end that they too might be well grounded and walk circumspectly in the truth.

Thus their handling of money will be in alignment with the life of God in them. Living with joyful conviction of glorifying God in all their transactions.

Nothing can parallel this noble venture these heaven-called men are living for.

However, in order to do any lasting work in and with God's people, the servant of God must know the delicate balance that operates between the head (mind) and the heart of man and how to use the pulpit as a platform to bringing the saints into accurate balance between the two.

For example, on his personal encounter with Jesus as a preacher in Luke 19;8, Zachaeus, a rich Jew who had made so much money from an unbalanced relationship between his heart and head, could not resist his heart invasion by heaven, responded promptly by declaring an end to fraudulent practices (Lk19: 8 "And Zacchaeus stood, and said unto the Lord; Behold, Lord, the half of my goods I give to the poor; and if I have taken anything from any man by false accusation, I restore him fourfold.) and the beginning of generosity towards the poor. This happened because of his heart shift.

What this implies is that, true stewardship of the pulpit by God's servant should lead to the shift in heart of the saints, with the Spirit of God coming to take governmental role over the exploits of the head (mind). Putting it in another way the regenerated heart of the saints must provide vector quality for the scalar quantity of the exploits of our minds.

The head (mind) provides the common ground for all men (Christians and non- Christians) to transact and hob-nob in the market place and make most of the same. The regenerated heart of the saints however provides the unique privilege of using ours in ways not only pleasing to God but targeted at advancing His Kingdom.

So the saints are men whose hearts are enthroned by God, and heads explored for God.

MAXIMISING THE MARKET PLACE

Although we the saints are not of this world by content, but we still live in this world and carry out God's assignments in this present world that is hostile to all that is called God in Christ. To do this effectively, God's people must be taught how to maximize their involvements in the market place without being consumed by the forces that regulate this present age!

The Apostle of Christ told the church to work in order to make meaningful earning.

2Thessalonians 3:6 – 10,

Now we command you, brethren, in the name of our Lord Jesus Christ, that ye withdraw yourselves from every brother that walketh disorderly, and not after the tradition which he received of us.

For yourselves know how ye ought to follow us: for we behaved not ourselves disorderly among you;

Neither did we eat any man's bread for nought; but wrought with labour and travail night and day, that we might not be chargeable to any of you:

Not because we have not power, but to make ourselves an ensample unto you to follow us.

For even when we were with you, this we commanded you, that if any would not work, neither should he eat.

They also modelled for the saints, the principle of legitimacy of personal responsibility by working.

1 Thessalonians 2:9,

For you remember, brethren, our labour and travail, for labouring night and day, because we would not chargeable unto any of you, we preached unto you the gospel of God.

So getting involved in honest work of providing goods and or rendering services is to be embraced and maximised by Christians like other men.

However, if the saints are to be involved in commerce, they might as well do such with absolute regard for the values and principles that regulate and make for maximal productivity in life. Learning progressively what it takes to do well financially is a must for any wise man and for that matter the Christian who is set out not only to meet his legitimate needs but to prudently use his honest earnings in advancing God's righteous cause on earth. Doing this effectively demands making all the money one can licitly make, and growing the same.

EXPLORING UNIVERSAL LAWS AND PRINCIPLES

Certain laws and principles regulates the financial world and such must be explored by God's people if we're to maximize our interactions in the market place.

This is a neutral zone that doesn't differentiate between believers or unbelievers, all that matters are laws and principles that guide such.

Consider these scriptures:

Seest thou a man diligent in his business? he shall stand before kings; he shall not stand before mean men. (Proverbs 22:29)

The hand of the diligent shall bear rule: but the slothful shall be under tribute. (Proverbs 12:24)

A faithful man shall abound with blessings: but he that maketh haste to be rich shall not be innocent. (Proverbs 28:20)

Better is little with the fear of the Lord than great treasure and trouble therewith. (Proverbs 15:16)

Through wisdom is a house builded, and by understanding it is established. Any enterprise is built by wise planning, becomes strong through common sense, and profits wonderfully by keeping abreast of the facts. (Proverbs 24:3-4)

Love not sleep, lest thou come to poverty; open thine eyes, and thou shalt be satisfied with bread. (Proverbs 20:13)

The soul of the sluggard desireth, and hath nothing: but the soul of the diligent shall be made fat. (Proverbs 13:4)

The sluggard is wiser in his own conceit than seven men that can render a reason. (Proverbs 26:16)

There is treasure to be desired and oil in the dwelling of the wise; but a foolish man spendeth it up. (Proverbs 21:20)

From the above scriptures and many more in the bible, it's obvious that God in His gracious design of life has put certain laws in place that guide our common existence, such that when such is embraced by any, productivity and financial fruitfulness will be the harvest.

The reality is that any man in Christ will find it pleasurable to embrace and function in these laws. In other words, teaching our members true Christianity will naturally make them to embrace diligence, patience, faithfulness, thoughtfulness, creativity, critical thinking, simplicity, thrift, friendliness, and stewardship.

As such, true believers will be among most productive and resourceful men. Shinning as light in the market place from transformed hearts becomes synergistic with our functional head.

Hence, quality of life from our hearts shape and dictate how we handle the quantities from our heads (minds).

Standing aloof in the market place or simply put separatism should not be found with us as God's people. We are skillfully and heartily getting involved in work place life as good stewards of God's resources.

FINANCIAL STEWARDSHIP

Like everything given to us freely by God to be stewarded even our very life, money and all it can bring to the saints must not just be made, multiplied and managed astutely in order to be financially relevant, we do ours as responsible citizens of God's kingdom.

We do not only embrace simplicity and soberness, we're ruthlessly altruistic and understated in all ours in order that God's resources are not used to fund our unbridled lusts and insatiable appetites! Using God's resources to fund our personal ego and self-projection manifesting in externalisms is constantly dealt with as the cross of Jesus apply its deliverance on our soul.

As such, as men who constantly experience inner freedom from the brutal enslavement by this present world system of materialism and vain externalism; Circumspectly, we prudently and God-fearingly use our resources in ways that reflect submission to the government of Christ in our hearts.

Such a beautiful and soul-enthralling experience is profitable for us as God's own consecrated people. Never again will anyone of God's people under our watch become waster of the blessed privilege given to the saints in Christ to steward God's financial resources entrusted to them!

TRUE RICHES OUR GAIN

As faithful and wise stewards of the Gospel, we must teach and train God's people the wise and balance ways to relate with money without being overtaken with the deceitfulness of riches or becoming irresponsible in the issues of life.

Believers must know the true riches in Christ they are called to pursue and progressively possess.

1 Timothy 6:10-11,

For the love of money is the root of all evil: which while some coveted after, they have erred from the faith, and pierced themselves through with many sorrows.

But thou, O man of God, flee these things; and follow after righteousness, godliness, faith, love, patience, meekness.

One of the greatest mistakes we can make is to teach the gospel of Christ with the mind that God's people might become financially rich, this is a subtle error that'll subvert the soul of the saints. While believers need money like others, the gospel is never to give the saints any advantage as it pertains to the quantities of this present life.

God's people must know that earthly riches are temporal and uncertain (1 Timothy 6:17) and do not form the basis of our success in life and ministry. While the magnanimous God has freely given to us all things to enjoy, the saints must know that possessing and enjoying such is not the goal nor the measure of the Christian faith.

Believers must be armed with the truth of the scriptures continually and should see to it that at no time are we swayed from the truth to begin to think and walk like the gentiles in the vanity of their minds.

1 Peter 1:18,

Forasmuch as ye know that ye were not redeemed with corruptible things, as silver and gold, from your vain conversation received by tradition from your fathers.

We're not saved by silver and gold; neither are we saved for it nor must we be measured by it. Our awareness of deceitfulness of riches protect us from being trapped in vain materialism like the Laodicean church in Revelation 3:17.

The wisdom of the scriptures informs our judgment in all our dealings with things earthly. Imagine the church of God at Smyna (Revelation 2:8); said to be poor in human judgment but to God, that was a truly rich church, as against the Laodicean church that was consumed with the plenty of earthly riches and as such became complacent. However, the Master described them as poor, miserable, wretched, naked and blind.

How the church need to rediscover the true riches in Christ and allow such to shape and govern how we relate with and handle our unique situations and circumstances. So that like Paul the apostle, we can truly say we know how to abase and abound by the inner workings of Christ. As kings in Christ, we reign in life over lack and plenty. In lack, we do not despair, complain and become bitter. In plenty, we are overcharged with surfeiting neither are we deluded to think that the quantities of this life is the testimonies of our personal walk with God.

To us gain is not godliness neither lack holiness. The true riches in Christ is our gain and such possession informs and shape how we relate with and handle the possessions and positions of this life to the glory of our King.

Chapter Four

THE 'NEVERS' OF THE PULPIT

Perverse disputings of men of corrupt minds, and destitute of the truth, supposing that gain is godliness: from such withdraw thyself. (I Timothy 6:5)

But have renounced the hidden things of dishonesty, not walking in craftiness, nor handling the word of God deceitfully, but by the manifestation of the truth commending ourselves to everyman's conscience in the sight of God. (2 Corinthians 4:2)

Today, for his unbridled and unconquered desire for wealth, Balaam continues to be a warning example to all of us as regards being circumspect with the way we use the blessed privilege of standing as God's servant. This prophet of God was drawn by inordinate gain though such came at the expense of the interest of the One he represented, yet the lust for inordinate wealth overpowered the resolve of this longstanding servant of God!

And Balaam answered and said unto the servants of Balak, If Balak would give me his house full of silver and gold, I cannot go beyond the word of the Lord my God, to do less or more. (Numbers 22:18)

Having eyes full of adultery, and that cannot cease from sin; beguiling unstable souls: an heart they have exercised with covetous practices; cursed children:

Which have forsaken the right way, and are gone astray, following the way of Balaam the son of Bosor, who loved the wages of unrighteousness. (2 Peter 2:14-15)

If what happened to this servant of God is written down in the scriptures is for our example and learning, it behooves us to be extremely chary in the way we use the sacred platform given to us to preach the timeless gospel of Christ.

Knowing also the warfare that exists between light and darkness, and how Satan longs to use the legists to lure the saints into error, for any minster to throw caution into the wind is to be extremely careless.

In the temptations Jesus faced, bowing down to worship Satan in order to gain the whole world was one (Matthew 4:8-9). Yet the Master declined the offer saying with his action that nothing on earth is worth replacing is unalloyed devotion to the worship of God and commitment to the praise of his glory!

However, looking at the way a lot of us ministers of the gospel operate and function behind the pulpit, it's as if nothing is at stake, and that money is everything.

Many of the warnings, advice, instructions and examples the prophets, Jesus and his apostles gave are being ignored or downplayed all because our morbid lust for money and all it can bring!

That there is something called deceitfulness of riches is totally oblivious to many of us, hence the kind of lifestyle we and our members live outside before the unregenerate.

Knowing fully well that what proceeds from us through the pulpit will shape the lives and lifestyles of our members and all our hearers in a way that is far-reaching than we can imagine.

1 Timothy 4:12,

Let no man despise thy youth; but be thou an example of the believers, in word, in conversation, in charity, in spirit, in faith, in purity.

Isaiah 9:16,

For the leaders of this people cause them to err; and they that are led of them are destroyed.

To say therefore that every pulpit must then be protected with "Nevers" will not be unnecessary carefulness.

Amongst the "Nevers" to be embraced are just these few that would be considered in this book

NEVER USE THE PULPIT FOR PERSONNAL GAIN

Nobody works for nothing, we're all driven by financial reward as we get involved in one legitimate work or the other and this is true in the scriptures.

Proverbs 4:23,

Keep thy heart with all diligence; for out of it are the issues of life.

Proverbs 13:11b,

Wealth gotten by vanity shall be diminished: but he that gathereth by labour shall increase.

However, the minister of the gospel must know the uniqueness of his assignment and the biblical reward of such.

Like the Levites in the Old Testament who were to see Jehovah as their inheritance, the minister of the gospel should see Christ and the advance of His cause in the world as their gain. i.e. feeding the flock of God, winning the lost, modelling Christ-centered life must be our drive and gain and not money.

1 Peter 5:2 says,

Feed the flock of God which is among you, taking the oversight thereof, not by constraint, but willingly; not for filthy lucre, but of a ready mind.

Paul declared, *'that I might win Christ'*. (Philippians 3:8)

1 Thessalonians 2:19-20,

For what is our hope, or joy, or crown of rejoicing? Are not even ye in the presence of our Lord Jesus Christ at his coming? For ye are our glory and joy.

1 Thessalonians 3:8,

For now we live, if ye stand fast in the Lord.

However, because the minister of the gospel is a human being with human needs – God has put structure in place to meet such. Through the works of his hands (Acts 20: 34. 2 Thessalonians 3:8) and the generous giving of the church (1 Corinthians 9:7-14)

Who goeth a warfare any time at his own charges? who planteth a vineyard, and eateth not of the fruit thereof? or who feedeth a flock, and eateth not of the milk of the flock?

Say I these things as a man? or saith not the law the same also?

For it is written in the law of Moses, Thou shalt not muzzle the mouth of the ox that treadeth out the corn. Doth God take care for oxen?

Or saith he it altogether for our sakes? For our sakes, no doubt, this is written: that he that ploweth should plow in hope; and that he that thresheth in hope should be partaker of his hope.

If we have sown unto you spiritual things, is it a great thing if we shall reap your carnal things?

If others be partakers of this power over you, are not we rather? Nevertheless we have not used this power; but suffer all things, lest we should hinder the gospel of Christ.

Do ye not know that they which minister about holy things live of the things of the temple? and they which wait at the altar are partakers with the altar?

Even so hath the Lord ordained that they which preach the gospel should live of the gospel. (1 Corinthians 9:7-14)

Let the elders that rule well be counted worthy of double honour, especially they who labour in the word and doctrine. (1 Timothy 5:17)

And certain women, which had been healed of evil spirits and infirmities, Mary called Magdalene, out of whom went seven devils,

And Joanna the wife of Chuza Herod's steward, and Susanna, and many others, which ministered unto him of their substance. (Luk8:2-3)

But it must be understood that supply of this continually in increasing measure are not the gain of God's servant but means to sustain us and keep us from worries of life while we're in relentless pursuit of the Master's pleasure.

Again let me reiterate this, the reward of any servant of God is not money or at all it can bring (i.e. good cars, houses, auditoria, landed properties, jet, etc.). All these things are means of empowering us to serve God in progressive measures.

Your true gain in the now are the transformed lives in Christ and your ultimate reward awaits you on the other side when the true Judge will assess all our works under His perfect light 1Cor3:13 (Every man's work shall be made manifest: for the day shall declare it, because it shall be revealed by fire; and the fire shall try every man's work of what sort it is)

Till then, let's keep laboring with purity of motives and motivations.

1 Corinthians 4:5,

Therefore, judge nothing before the time, until the Lord come, who both will bring to light the hidden things of darkness, and will make manifest the counsels of the hearts: and then shall every man have praise of God.

NEVER COMPROMISE THE TRUTH REGARDLESS OF THE GAIN

Getting stocked with the truth without compromise is one of the hardest things to do by mortals more so if there is obvious gain at stake. This reality impacts no one than the minister of the gospel who is continually barraged with the temptation of modifying, adding, removing, and exaggerating the truth for the present obvious gain in a world that measures any by the quantity of their possession and not the quality of their hearts.

2 Corinthians 5:12,

For we commend not ourselves again unto you, but give you occasion to glory on our behalf, that ye may have somewhat to answer them which glory in appearance, and not in heart.

The holy writ is replete with men who suffered rejection or lack, all because of their uncompromising allegiance to the truth. Like the apostles, they have chosen to renounce the hidden things of dishonesty (2 Corinthians 4:2) and embrace the conviction that the world to come is their blessed hope.

Looking for that blessed hope, and the glorious appearing of the great God and our Saviour Jesus Christ. (Titus 2:13)

Nevertheless, we, according to his promise, look for new heavens and a new earth, wherein dwelleth righteousness.

Wherefore, beloved, seeing that ye look for such things, be diligent that ye may be found of him in peace, without spot, and blameless. (2 Peter 3:13-14)

But where you have ministers who glory and measure themselves in earthly treasures, compromising the truth becomes a normal lifestyle.

Brethren, be followers together of me, and mark them which walk so as ye have us for an ensample.

(For many walk, of whom I have told you often, and now tell you even weeping, that they are the enemies of the cross of Christ:

Whose end is destruction, whose God is their belly, and whose glory is in their shame, who mind earthly things.) (Philippians 3:17-19)

Personally, I believe we ministers should see ourselves as privileged in being graced to purvey the timeless truth found exclusively in Christ and as such no material gain should come into play, how much more to pervert the truth for such unconscionable gain.

Knowing the meaning and experiencing the grace of being trusted with the gospel is more fulfilling and rewarding than anything earthly.

I Thessalonians 2:2-6,

But even after that we had suffered before, and were shamefully entreated, as ye know, at Philippi, we were bold in our God to speak unto you the gospel of God with much contention.

For our exhortation was not of deceit, nor of uncleanness, nor in guile:

But as we were allowed of God to be put in trust with the gospel, even so we speak; not as pleasing men, but God, which trieth our hearts.

For neither at any time used we flattering words, as ye know, nor a cloke of covetousness; God is witness:

Nor of men sought we glory, neither of you, nor yet of others, when we might have been burdensome, as the apostles of Christ.

The dearth of true meaning of our assignment and the end of it has made us easy prey to tyrannical control of financial gain.

Balaam the prophet of God, lost out in ministry because he compromised the truth about God's transaction with his people, when he was offered inordinate gain by Balak.

For I will promote thee unto very great honour, and I will do whatsoever thou sayest unto me: come therefore, I pray thee, curse me this people.

And Balaam answered and said unto the servants of Balak, If Balak would give me his house full of silver and gold, I cannot go beyond the word of the Lord my God, to do less or more. (Numbers22: 17-18)

2 Peter 2:15-16,

Which have forsaken the right way, and are gone astray, following the way of Balaam the son of Bosor, who loved the wages of unrighteousness;

But was rebuked for his iniquity: the dumb ass speaking with man's voice forbad the madness of the prophet.

Dear servants of God flee the love of money and be resolutely committed to living and preaching the truth regardless of the gain, so that you may stand before Him on that day without shame of having used all your lives to pursue vanity.

NEVER EXPLOIT THE ANOINTING FOR GAIN

I was in a meeting the other time and having spoken charismatically with a lot of motivation, the servant of God began to call people to make pledge N100,000; N50,000; N20,000. Somehow looking at the whole scenario, I wasn't comfortable, because I felt it was more of taking advantage of the vulnerability of the people after all that had happened. While I don't want to be the judge of such, it is common in our meetings and with certain servants of God that once they come to your meetings, money must be raised with so many promises from God.

Comparing ourselves with the apostles in the bible, somehow we seem to exploit the anointing given us to preach the gospel for financial gain than for the spiritual transformation of God's people.

Imagine, after a crusade, organized to win souls to the kingdom, yet in such meetings ministers of gospel will still call unbelievers out to give and make absurd pledges.

Sometime you wonder the wisdom and integrity of such transactions. Is it that they must pay for the miracle, their salvation, for the minister's welfare or logistics? To me, if we have to raise money at crusades or some specialized outreach programs, then such should not hold until we have the money otherwise we are presenting the kingdom of God in a bad light by our greed and carelessness. I guess the minister of the gospel should be sensitive to the collection of money. Elisha told Gehazi, is it time to receive money after Naman was healed of his leprosy?

2 Kings 5:26,

And he said unto him, went not mine heart with thee, when the man turned again from his chariot to meet thee? Is it a time to receive money, and to receive garments, and olive yards, and vineyards, and sheep, and oxen, and menservants, and maidservants?

Some of us will even raise money at an invitation given to us, in order for our honorarium to be much, how inordinate we are. Remember the all-seeing eyes of God is seeing us and by Him actions are weighed.

Some of us are always burdensome on our host, we come with unattainable demands all because we want to preach the gospel that somebody laid His life down for. We are so consumed with eating, pleasure and comfort that our host must pay by tasking all their members. How different we are from Jesus we represent and the examples modelled by His apostles.

Consider these scriptures!

Behold, the third time I am ready to come to you; and I will not be burdensome to you: for I seek not yours, but you: for the children ought not to lay up for the parents, but the parents for the children. (2 Corinthians 12:14)

Not that I speak in respect of want: for I have learned, in whatsoever state I am, therewith to be content.

I know both how to be abased, and I know how to abound: everywhere and in all things I am instructed both to be full and to be hungry, both to abound and to suffer need. (Philippians 4:11-12)

At other time, the burden we exert on our host is to go with hosts of men that have nothing to do with the message delivery. Your host comes under heavy burden in coping with the entourage that followed you.

I believe, it is only wise to inform one's host the number of people that will accompany you so that adequate preparation can be made if they can cope.

I believe every host should take care and give good hospitality to their invited guest, in a manner worthy of the Lord (3 John 5-6). If your church cannot take good care of God's servant, don't invite any until you're able and can do such responsibly.

Till then keep laboring faithfully and don't jump the gun thinking that there is one anointing somewhere that will grow your church or you want to associate with in order to build your own spiritual resume.

NEVER APPROVE MEN BASED ON EARTHLY POSITIONS OR POSSESSIONS

Doing all things for and from the kingdom gain is a tough decision a minister must always make when such is constantly confronted with the choice of earthly gain. Relating with and approving men based on earthly advantage is so easy for us to do as God's servant but as faithful servant, we must be circumspect and discreet in all our handlings.

My brethren, have not the faith of our Lord Jesus Christ, the Lord of glory, with respect of persons.

For if there come unto your assembly a man with a gold ring, in goodly apparel, and there come in also a poor man in vile raiment;

And ye have respect to him that weareth the gay clothing, and say unto him, sit thou here in a good place; and say to the poor, stand thou there, or sit here under my footstool:

Are ye not then partial in yourselves, and are become judges of evil thoughts?

Hearken, my beloved brethren, Hath not God chosen the poor of this world rich in faith, and heirs of the kingdom which he hath promised to them that love him?

But ye have despised the poor. Do not rich men oppress you, and draw you before the judgment seats? (James 2:1-6;9)

It is easier in our churches today, for the rich to climb the ladder of leadership than for the poor, though the poor might be more committed to Jesus. In any case, God chose most of us and we were groomed when we are in lack; so how come we are more pro-rich people. Evidently there is a slant in our hearts toward the glory of this world than the seeking the glory and pleasure of God.

Like Samuel who moved in the flesh and considered the height and countenance of Eliab, in the choice of King, but was rejected by God who chooses after men's heart.

And it came to pass, when they were come, that he looked on Eliab, and said, surely the Lord's anointed is before him. (1 Samuel 16:6-7)

We make choices after positions and possessions of men in order that they might be used to build our so called ministry and not God's kingdom nor His church.

Approving ourselves as God's ministers in the way we relate and handle men from the pulpit is so critical if we're not going to be an offence to the same cause we defend. Our relationship with men whether rich or poor, learned or unlearned, etc. must be a reflection of our allegiance to God's cause and our readiness to choose anyone qualified based on heart and true spirituality. Any form of partiality based on human advantages must be confronted and dealt with.

Let's not unwittingly constitute great problem to the cause of a kingdom that can and will do without us if not for the grace bestowed on us and such must not be carelessly or cunningly squandered. We must be able to tell the rich, 'your money perish with you', if such seem to be offering money for advantage with God.

Saying, give me also this power, that on whomsoever I lay hands, he may receive the Holy Ghost.

But Peter said unto him, thy money perish with thee, because thou hast thought that the gift of God may be purchased with money. (Act8:19-20)

Another word of caution to us fellow servants of God is promoting pastors of the branches of our church based on returns of offering and tithes. This is a great evil that is injurious to all.

In this kind of administration, you can bet it that God's Spirit will leave you to be running your personal business called churches. This has led to all manner of sharp practices among pastors; manipulations and coercions from the pulpit for people to give so that associate pastors can ultimately have good record before the senior pastor or general overseer.

My brethren these things ought not to be.

How we need to be delivered from measuring ourselves by money and numerical growth and pursue the true stand of men in Christ (1 Thessalonians 3:8).

It is time to function as wise and faithful stewards of the timeless truth.

NEVER IGNORE THE SOURCE OF THEIR INCOME

One man of God spoke confidently in one meeting, "I might not like the dirty job you're doing, but the money you're bringing to church is not dirty". To me, this look like utterance from a charlatan, for how can a man of God operate with this kind of mind frame and will be sane, obviously there is greedy love of money somewhere.

In Deuteronomy 23:18, God said, *'do not bring the hire of a whore or the price of dog into my house'*. The question is, is any money labelled "Hire of a Whore"? This leaves us with the fact that God is more concerned with the legitimacy of the work of our members than the money brought to church.

Paul said in Ephesians 4:28, *'Let him that stole steal no more, but rather let him labour, working with his hands the things which is good, that he may have to give to him that needeth'*.

Using our hands to do honest work matters to God than the money we make. Cutting corners, cheating on our organization, defrauding people, using underhanded methods, using sub-standard products in order to maximize profit, cheating on your employees by paying them unfairly (Jam1:16), prostitution, internet fraud, etc. all must be confronted and discouraged from the pulpit and not just rejoice at the money brought to the church and deliberately close our eyes to the source. We must show sincerity of concern for the uprightness and transformation of our members than the money they bring to church.

Imagine how many government officials and politicians have greedily defrauded this country and their states. Money that should have been used for our corporate good yet such fund found their ways into church through these men, only for you and I as their pastors to open-heartedly receive such outrageous giving, this is grave ungodliness from the pulpit. These are men that should be rebuked and warned of their corrupt practices that will jettison the growth of their country and ultimately bring shame to God's name.

Like the apostle Paul said in 2 Corinthians 12:14, *'for I seek not yours, but you'*. We too should be able to declare by our words and actions, we seek the conformity of our members to the image of Christ and the corresponding lifestyle that proceeds from their inner transformation and not the money they bring to church!

Having gone through this small book, it's evident that for us to make most of the ministry committed to our trust, we must circumspectly deal with money and all it can bring as good stewards of the mysteries of Christ.

My prayer is that may the good Lord who has called us into his vineyard grant us good grace to make necessary heart adjustments that will make us to relate and handle this means (money) to the end that true gospel of Christ is the only thing we're committed to preaching, teaching and living by.

Seeing men saved, become more like Christ and execute his pleasures on earth, our ultimate pursuits.

God bless you!

82

About the Author

Dr 'Laide Odusote is a contemporary but passionate 'God-Chaser' who defines life ONLY by how much he knows God, how much of Christ rules in his heart and how much he lives for God's pleasure by faith.

Olaide has indeed been a recipient of God's grace in many ways. He's a medical doctor by training, former University lecturer, a school proprietor and a father of three.

He's currently the lead pastor of Integrity Worship Centre with centres in Sagamu, Ogun state and Lagos state, Nigeria.

He's currently in Edmonton, Alberta, Canada to pioneer the takeoff of Integrity Worship Centre (The Exchange Centre).

He has a mandate of raising a Christ-centred people ('ChristoBassadors')

Pastor Laide is a true Christian leader, exemplifying and teaching all around to commit to a life of unending conformation to Christ. His knowledge of scriptures is inspiring, his depth in theology and doctrinal reasoning is compelling. His passion for prayers, submission to Christ, commitment to feeding God's people and rugged discipleship is relentless.

With unyielding zeal, he's constantly sharing his knowledge that everyone may fully come to understand the true intent of the scriptures.

May you be richly blessed, encouraged and perfected by the ministry of this servant of God.

www.ingramcontent.com/pod-product-compliance
Lightning Source LLC
Chambersburg PA
CBHW071944120726
48001CB00005B/2029